Unit 1 · Dividing into teams

1.1 Early tensions, 1945–1947

Source 1

A Soviet war-time poster. The caption says 'Avenge our people's grief'.

МСТИ ЗА ГОРЕ НАРОДА!

During the Second World War the United States, the Soviet Union and the United Kingdom were allies: the 'Big Three'. Their leaders, Roosevelt, Stalin and Churchill, met several times, for example at Teheran and Yalta. They discussed the conduct of the war and also reached agreements about what would happen after it was over.

But by the end of 1949 the United States and the Soviet Union were enemies. They faced each other across a divided Europe, each equipped with nuclear weapons. From then until 1991 the two superpowers fought a 'Cold War' in which they competed to develop their nuclear arsenals and win support from other countries. Their rivalry even extended into space, as they raced to be the first to put people into orbit and reach the moon. How did these war-time comrades become enemies? How did their rivalry begin?

The Soviet experience of war

The Germans invaded the Soviet Union in June 1941. A Russian who was a child at the time later described the effects:

Source 2

From Raisa Gorbachev's memoirs, *I Hope*, written in 1991. Her husband was the Soviet Union's last leader.

Millions of lives lost, millions of lives ruined. Houses laid waste, families orphaned, towns and villages destroyed, scorched earth . . .. Faces swollen from hunger. And the feeling of fear – of losing your food ration card or your bread ration. I remember it to this very day. And gleaning the fields for ears of grain and frozen potatoes. That is the way it was.

The city of Leningrad (now St Petersburg) suffered particularly badly. The Germans laid a siege which lasted nearly 900 days. Nearly a million people died there, of injuries, cold, hunger, disease. This was more than the USA lost during the whole of the war.

During those terrible years Stalin tried to persuade his allies, Britain and the USA, to attack the Germans from the west. This 'Second Front' would take the pressure off the Soviet people. But the Western Allies refused to attack until they were ready. Stalin thought they were delaying on purpose to allow the Germans time to destroy the Soviet Union.

In February 1943 the Soviet Red Army defeated a German army at Stalingrad. In August the biggest tank battle of the war, involving 2.7 million men, ended with the defeat of the German Panzer divisions. These battles were the turning point of the war in Europe. The Red Army drove the Germans out of Soviet territory and back across Eastern Europe. In April 1945 the Red Army captured Berlin.

The Soviet people were exhausted by the war. Their economy was ruined. At least 27 million citizens had lost their lives.

■ Look at Source 1. Do you think the Russian people are likely to have wanted 'revenge' after the war? If so, were they justified?

The Soviet take-over of Eastern Europe

In 1945 the 'Big Three' signed the 'Yalta Declaration on Liberated Europe'. It said that people should have the right to choose their governments. But Stalin wanted to control Eastern Europe in order to ensure that the Soviet Union could not be invaded again. He was willing to hold elections so that governments would appear to be democratic. But he made sure they were pro-communist. In the West, the Americans interfered behind the scenes to stop Communists being elected to the governments of Italy and France. Stalin did not object. He thought that if he let the Allies do what they wanted in Western Europe, they would give him a free hand in the East.

Source 3

The 'Big Three', Churchill, Roosevelt and Stalin, share a joke at the Yalta Conference in 1945. Roosevelt was ill and died shortly afterwards.

Churchill's view

Churchill was appalled by Stalin's actions. In 1946 he made a famous speech, declaring that an 'iron curtain' had descended across Europe. He said that all the countries behind that line:

Source 4

From a speech Winston Churchill made at Fulton, USA, 5 March 1946.

. . . lie in what I must call the Soviet sphere. And all are subject to a very high measure of control from Moscow.

The American President did not agree with Churchill's view. But Stalin took the speech as evidence of a new Anglo–American alliance threatening the Soviet Union. He retorted angrily that:

Source 5

From a speech Stalin made on 13 March 1946, in reply to Churchill.

The Soviet Union's loss of life has been several times greater than that of Britain and the USA put together . . . . So what is so surprising about the Soviet Union, anxious for its future safety, trying to see that loyal governments should exist in these countries?

Key

◼ areas taken over by USSR 1939 onwards

▨ area of Germany given to Poland in 1945 to compensate for land taken by USSR

‥‥‥ pre-war boundaries

— the 'Iron Curtain'

Source 6

How Europe was divided between 1945 and 1947.

The impact of the war on the United States

The United States' war experience differed from that of the Soviet Union. There was no fighting on American soil, no bombing of American cities. By 1945 it was a superpower and the world's richest nation.

Truman, President Roosevelt's successor, distrusted the Soviets. He said that:

Source 7

Truman made this remark to a visitor in April 1945.

. . . the Russians would soon be put in their place and the United States would then take the lead in running the world the way the world ought to be run.

Stalin, angered by Truman's attitude, wanted the West to consider the Soviet Union's security. In fact the West thought the Red Army provided the Soviet Union with more than enough security. The Americans claimed in 1946 that there were 2.5 million Soviet troops in Europe. One of Truman's advisors wrote:

Source 8

From an article published in 1947 and signed 'X'. The writer was George Kennan, an American expert on Soviet affairs.

. . . it is clear that the main element of any United States policy towards the Soviet Union must be that of a long-term, patient but firm . . . containment.

Question

a) Why was the West fearful of the Soviet Union by 1947?

b) Why was Stalin suspicious of the West?

1.2   US intervention in Europe and its effect on East–West relations, 1947–1955

The policy of containment

After the war Britain sent troops to help the Greek government fight a civil war against republican rebels, many of them communist. By 1947 the British could not afford to continue. They pulled out, leaving the Americans to take over. Advisors warned Truman that if Greece became communist, Italy and France would follow. Truman adopted Kennan's idea of a 'policy of containment'. He told Congress:

Source 9

From a speech by President Truman in April 1947. These ideas also became known as the 'Truman Doctrine'.

Totalitarian regimes Governments forced on people against their will. **Subjugation** Control.

The peoples of a number of countries . . . have recently had totalitarian regimes forced upon them . . . .

I believe it must be the policy of the United States to support free people who are resisting attempted subjugation by armed minorities or outside pressures . . . .

If we falter . . . we may endanger the peace of the world – and we shall surely endanger the welfare of our own nation.

This speech persuaded Congress to vote in favour of financing military aid to Greece.

The Marshall Plan

Britain was not the only country with economic problems. Much of Europe was still suffering from the effects of the war. A member of the US government reported that:

Source 10

From a report by Will Clayton, US Under Secretary of State, who toured Europe in May 1947.

Millions of people in the cities are slowly starving . . .. Without prompt and substantial aid from the United States, economic, social and political disintegration will overwhelm Europe.

This worried the Americans. Exports to Europe were worth $15 billion a year. They could not afford to lose this market. They also feared that desperation might drive people to support the Communists. Truman decided that the United States had to help Europe:

Source 11

From a speech made on Truman's behalf in May 1947.

It is necessary if we are to preserve our own freedoms . . . necessary for our national security. And it is our duty and privilege as human beings.

The US Secretary of State, George Marshall, drew up a plan to rebuild Europe's economy. A key element was the recovery of Germany. Its coal and steel were essential to European industry. Although the Soviets were afraid of German revival, Stalin at first seemed to want to join the Plan. He sent 89 experts to a conference to discuss it in 1947. However, the United States did not want Soviet participation. They set conditions they knew Stalin would not accept. The Soviets withdrew from the talks. Stalin ordered the East European countries not to join the Marshall Plan.

1   What reasons does Truman give in Source 9 for the policy of containment?

2   What reasons do Sources 10 and 11 give for the Marshall Plan?

This British cartoon of 1947 shows Truman building a barrier out of dollars to stop communism entering Western Europe.

■ What does the cartoon suggest was the link between the policy of containment and the Marshall Plan?

Truman asked Congress for $17 billion to finance the Plan. This led to tremendous arguments. These were still going on in 1948 when Communists overthrew the Czechoslovak government. Truman told Congress that the United States must meet this threat to the very survival of freedom. They voted through the Marshall Plan.

The Berlin blockade, 1948–1949

In 1945 the Allies divided Germany between them. Berlin, the capital, lay in the Soviet zone and that too was divided. So the Western Allies had a foothold in the East.

By 1948 the Western Allies had merged their zones. Money provided by the Marshall Plan was rebuilding German industry. The prospect of a prosperous, united West Germany alarmed the Soviets. In 1948 the West introduced a common currency and tried to circulate it in Berlin. That was the last straw. In July Moscow ordered that all road and rail links between Berlin and West Germany should be cut.

The Governor of the American zone proposed that an armed convoy should force its way down the autobahn (motorway) to Berlin. Truman rejected that idea. Instead he authorised an airlift to fly supplies into the city. It was risky: an incident could have resulted in war. But it worked. In May 1949 Stalin ordered the lifting of the blockade.

The establishment of NATO

The Berlin blockade enabled Truman to persuade Congress that the United States should join an alliance against the USSR. In 1949 America and eleven other countries set up the North Atlantic Treaty Organisation. The Treaty stated:

From the North Atlantic Treaty, 1949.

. . . the Parties . . . will maintain and develop their individual and collective capacity to resist armed attack.

The Parties agree that an armed attack against one or more of them . . . shall be considered an attack against them all.

Some Americans questioned this agreement. Why not use the UN to provide support if there was an attack? Would America have to send troops to Europe? People were still protesting over that when, in September, Truman announced that the Soviets had exploded an atomic bomb. The USSR had become a superpower.

Growing Soviet fears

Truman described the policy of containment and the Marshall Plan as two halves of the same walnut. He did not say they were aimed against the Soviet Union but the Soviets believed they were. They thought the West might use its economic strength and monopoly of the bomb to destroy the USSR (see Source 14).

Source 14

A 'Top Secret' map of possible Soviet targets produced by the British in 1949.

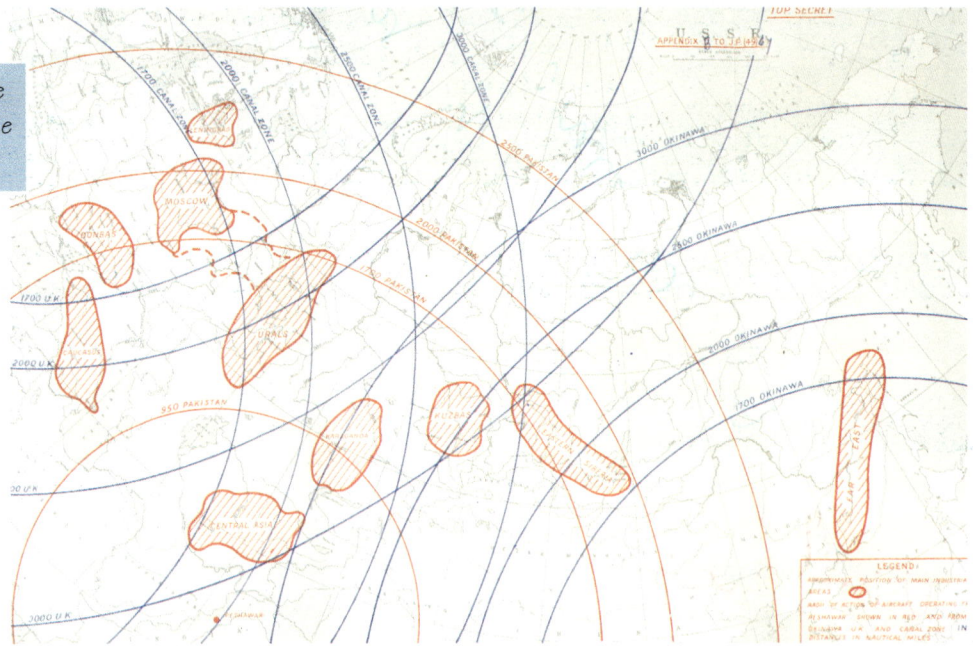

1 What does this 'Top Secret' map suggest about the relationship between Britain and the USA?

2 Do you think the Soviet Union was justified in its fears of the West? Use the Sources and any other information you have in your answer.

The Soviet reaction and the Warsaw Pact

In 1949 the Soviets responded to the Marshall Plan. They set up their own East European economic union, called COMECON. Meanwhile there were still tensions over Germany. The West and the Soviet Union were committed to reunifying Germany, but they could not agree on how to go about it. In May 1955 West Germany was formally admitted to NATO. Once again Germany was a military power. The Soviets had been afraid of this. Now the East European countries signed the Warsaw Pact. Like NATO, this was intended to be a defensive alliance. But it was run from Moscow and used to keep control in Eastern Europe. The Soviet Prime Minister said:

Source 15

From *The Times*' report of the Soviet Prime Minister's statement about the Warsaw Pact, 12 May 1955.

. . . the best way to ensure peace and prevent new aggression . . . is the organisation of a system of collective security . . . .

. . . the threat to the security of our states as a result of the aggressive measures of the western Powers, requires . . . new measures for strengthening the defences of our peace-loving countries. The treaty of friendship, co-operation and mutual aid . . . is precisely to serve these aims.

How do the purposes of NATO and the Warsaw Pact compare, according to Sources 13 and 15?

So, by 1955, East and West had formed two alliances, NATO and the Warsaw Pact, headed by the two superpowers and divided by the 'Iron Curtain'.

Task

Choose either the USA or the USSR. Look back through Unit 1. Make a list of the incidents which created tensions from 1945 and 1955 from your superpower's point of view. You could use the list to write an explanation of why the superpowers became enemies. Or you could design a comic strip showing how tensions grew from the viewpoint of your superpower.

Unit 2 · Containment in action: Korea

2.1   How did Korea become a Cold War battleground?

Source 1

The 'Domino Theory'.

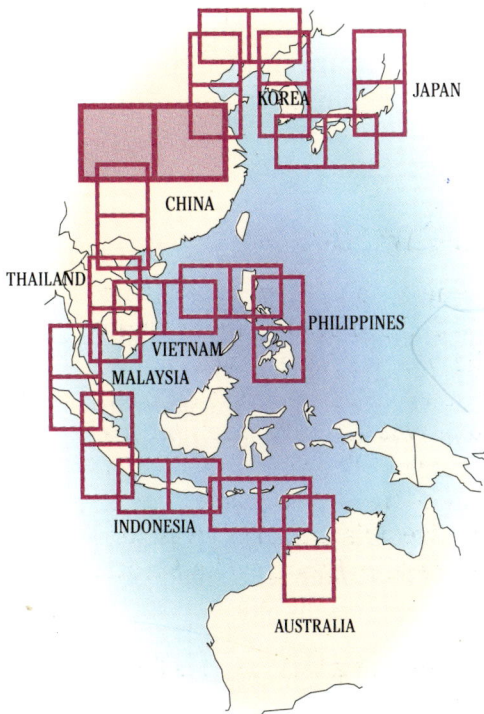

The Cold War had begun in Europe. But George Kennan warned that the Russians aimed at world conquest. In 1949 the Communists took power in China. This heightened American fears. They thought that if communism took hold in one country, neighbouring countries would fall to communist forces, like a row of dominoes (Source 1). Now communism had to be contained world-wide, not just in Europe.

The division of Korea

At the end of the Second World War the United States and Soviet Union agreed to a temporary division of Korea. But they could not agree about reuniting the country. By 1948 separate governments had been set up. Kim Il Sung was supported by the Soviet Union in the North and Syngman Rhee backed by the USA in the South. Both leaders claimed to represent Korea as a whole. In 1950 the North Koreans unexpectedly invaded the South. They captured the capital, Seoul, and drove the South Koreans right down to the south.

The United Nations and Korea

The USA decided that this example of communist expansion must be resisted. In New York the Soviets were boycotting the UN because of its refusal to recognise the new government in China. That meant the US could get resolutions through the Security Council to send UN troops to Korea. In September they landed at Inchon and recaptured Seoul. A war reporter followed the Marines into the city and described what he saw:

Source 2

From a report by Rutherford Poats, war correspondent for the American United Press Agency, in September 1950

. . . on this street corner was condensed the full horror of war . . . . A young woman poked among the charred timbers for her possessions, or perhaps for her child . . . . A tiny figure . . . stumbled down the street. Her face, arms and legs were burned and almost eaten away by an American white phosphorous shell. She was blind, but somehow alive. She was about the size of my little girl.

Fifty thousand North Koreans were killed and the rest fled back across the border. This should have meant the end of the fighting. It didn't. On 7 October the UN passed a new resolution authorising the overthrow of North Korea. UN troops, led by an American, General MacArthur, crossed the border. They marched north towards China. Kim Il Sung sent pleas for help to both Stalin and Mao. Mao, the new Chinese leader, was afraid that the West might attack China. He could not afford to risk open war with the United States. So he ordered 'volunteers' to enter Korea. Stalin waited to see what would happen.

Key

■ area captured during North Korean invasion, 1950
→ UN forces advance, 1950
→ Chinese attacks, Dec 1950
— the two sides 'dug-in', 1951–1953
✈ 'Mig alley' – the Soviet fighter aircraft route
— the 1953 cease-fire line

Source 3

Korean refugees watching US trucks. A million people fled their homes in the early stages of the war.

Source 4

Korea during the war, 1950–1953.

Faced with the unexpected appearance of 140,000 Chinese troops, UN forces pulled back. By Christmas the Chinese had driven them out of North Korea and captured Seoul. As the UN withdrew, Soviet fighter aircraft appeared over North Korea. On 8 November the world's first ever all-jet air battle took place between American and Soviet planes.

The USA and USSR at war

By March 1951, UN troops had managed to fight their way back to the 38th Parallel. There both sides 'dug in'. Any attempt to advance resulted in huge casualties. There was stalemate on the ground, so the United States tried to win the war using air power. As peace talks dragged on, American planes remorselessly attacked North Korea with high explosives and napalm. A British reporter described the effect:

Source 5

A British journalist, James Cameron, recorded this report for the BBC, but it was not broadcast.

Over the scene of silent desolation crept a reassuring smell that immediately took me back to Sunday dinners in Britain: the smell of roast pork. For that's what a napalmed human being smells like.

Soviet pilots helped the Chinese Air Force. They wore Chinese uniforms and their planes had Chinese markings. American leaders knew the Soviets were fighting but kept it secret. An official explained later :

Source 6

One of President Eisenhower's advisors talking to Jon Halliday, a British historian, in the early 1990s.

We had to keep that under the carpet. If that had ever gotten out, there would have been tremendous pressure to have a war with Russia.

For two years the Americans and Soviets fought each other. The United States lost 3,500 planes, the Soviet Union about 2,800. The world knew nothing about it.

Soviet involvement in Korea led Truman to consider a direct attack on the Soviet Union. In January 1952 he wrote in his diary:

Source 7

Jon Halliday 'Secret war of the Top Guns', an article published in 1992.

It seems to me that the proper approach now would be an ultimatum with a 10-day expiration limit [to] Moscow . . .. This means all-out war . . .. Moscow, St Petersburg, Vladivostock, Peking, Shanghai and every manufacturing plant in China and the Soviet Union will be eliminated . . .. This is the final chance for the Soviet government to decide whether it wishes to survive or not.

The North Koreans were forced underground by the air attacks. They made themselves shelters to live in and even built underground factories. Urban areas became 'cities of chimneys' since only the chimneys withstood the bombs. The air raids killed 2 million people and injured many more.

By the time Eisenhower took office as President of the United States in January 1953, the two sides were exhausted. In March Stalin died. The new leaders of both the United States and the Soviet Union wanted peace. On 27 July the UN, China and North Korea signed an armistice. American efforts to 'contain' communism switched to Vietnam (see Unit 5).

Source 8

Survivors amongst the rubble after an American bombardment.

Questions

1   Read Source 6. What might have been the outcome if the Americans had not kept the Soviet Union's involvement 'under the carpet'?

2   Would President Truman have been justified in launching 'all-out war' on the Soviet Union?

3   Use Source 1 to explain why the USA used so much force in Korea.

2.2   How has the Korean War been portrayed?

Source 9

From a TV documentary about the way wars are reported, by John Pilger, who has often written for the *Guardian* and *Observer* newspapers.

Reports of the Korean War were tightly controlled, by governments and by news film-makers and newspaper publishers. People did not know the Soviet Air Force was fighting. They did not realise that both Truman and Eisenhower considered using atomic bombs. A British writer has claimed:

It was a racist war and many correspondents were under instructions to play down the suffering of the Korean people. Instead the war was reported . . . as a 'Boys' Own Annual' saga of good versus evil.

That view has tended to find its way into text-books:

Source 10

Brian Catchpole, *A Map History of the Modern World*, first published in 1968. This text-book was widely used in schools in the 1970s and Eighties.

So, under the banner of the United Nations, troops from sixteen nations came to Korea – and in the nick of time for the Communists were already threatening Pusan!
    . . . the UN commander was the famous US general MacArthur. He decided to strike the Communists in the rear and ordered the successful Inchon landings in September. Soon the UN troops had captured Seoul amidst hideous slaughter and they reached the 38th Parallel. Their task, it seemed, was accomplished. The Communists had been contained. But the Americans were determined to destroy the aggressor state; only with the destruction of North Korea, they argued, could the people of Korea be united.

Questions

1 Study Sources 2 and 5.
a) What similarities are there in these two journalists' descriptions?
b) What effect do you think these descriptions were intended to have on the public?

2 Compare the photographs, Sources 3 and 8. In each case, what aspect of the war is the photographer trying to show? Which one would you choose to illustrate your own account of the war and why?

3 Read Sources 9 and 10.
a) Do you think that the war was a 'saga of good versus evil' or not? Pick out words and phrases from Source 10 to support your view.
b) Can you suggest why the author of a school text-book might write in this way?

4 Sources 2, 3, 5 and 8 do show some of the Korean people's sufferings. Does that mean John Pilger (Source 9) is wrong when he says that reporters were told to play them down? Explain your answer.

Task

Look back through Unit 2 and pick out any information you can about how the war affected the Korean people themselves. Use it to write an account of the Korean War from the point of view of the Korean people.

Unit 3 · The arms race, 1945-1960

The rivalry between the superpowers was reflected in an 'arms race' between them. The two sides competed to create ever larger stockpiles of weapons and military hardware. How far was this competition to build weapons of mass destruction to blame for increasing tensions?

3.1 Hiroshima: the opening shot

On 6 August 1945 a US bomber dropped an atomic weapon on the Japanese city of Hiroshima. A survivor remembers:

Source 1

Katoaka Osamu was a schoolboy in Hiroshima when the bomb fell.

. . . a flash. It was indescribable. It was as if a monstrous piece of celluloid had flared up all at once. Even as my eyes were being pierced by the sharp red flash, the school building was already crumbling.

Hiroshima has been called the opening shot in the Cold War. The United States claimed that it dropped the bomb in 1945 to end the war quickly and with fewer casualties. But that may not have been the only reason. In 1960 the US Secretary of State admitted that he had wanted to end the war with Japan before the Soviets became involved. Besides, developing the atomic bomb had been so expensive that the Americans wanted to see how it worked.

Source 2

The effect of the bomb on Hiroshima.

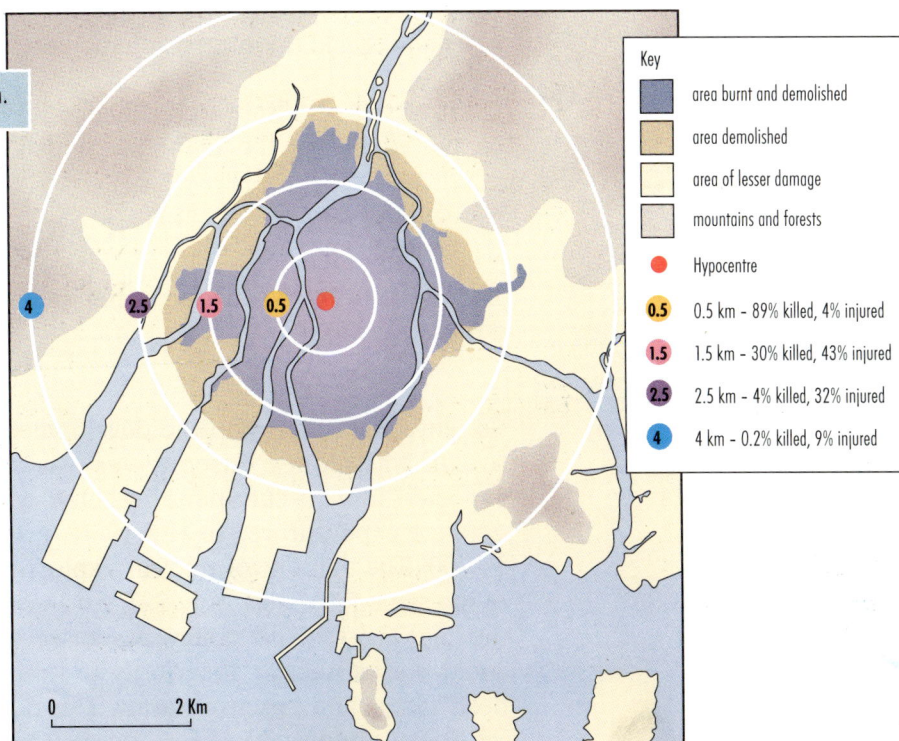

Key
- area burnt and demolished
- area demolished
- area of lesser damage
- mountains and forests
- ● Hypocentre
- 0.5 0.5 km – 89% killed, 4% injured
- 1.5 1.5 km – 30% killed, 43% injured
- 2.5 2.5 km – 4% killed, 32% injured
- 4 4 km – 0.2% killed, 9% injured

0   2 Km

What do you think of Stalin's response to Hiroshima? Do you think this response was justified?

Stalin thought the West had used the bomb to intimidate the Russians. He ordered Soviet scientists to press ahead with a Soviet bomb. He tripled their pay and started pouring money into atomic research. These efforts paid off in 1949 when the Soviets tested an A bomb in Siberia.

3.2   The 1950s: Eisenhower versus Khrushchev

Source 3

An American H bomb test in the Pacific in 1956. Both sides caused serious contamination with such tests.

In 1953 power changed hands in the United States and the Soviet Union. Both the new leaders, President Eisenhower and Mr Khrushchev, had been soldiers during the Second World War. They knew from their own experience the suffering and devastation caused by war. They wanted to reduce tension to lessen the risk of another one. But despite their efforts to achieve peaceful coexistence, when Eisenhower left office in 1960 relations were worse than ever. Why?

The race for 'strategic superiority'

Once both sides had the A bomb, they wanted more effective weapons systems which would give them an advantage. This was called 'strategic superiority'. After the Soviets tested their atom bomb both sides started work on an even more powerful weapon: the hydrogen bomb. The A bomb was far more destructive than any weapon ever known before. Yet both sides were racing to develop an even more dangerous device. Why? To gain strategic superiority. In March 1954 the USA tested six H bombs in the Pacific. In November 1955 the Soviets tested a very similar device. The two sides were neck and neck.

Why bombs instead of armies?

Both leaders were aware of the terrible dangers of nuclear weapons. Eisenhower had opposed using the bomb against the Japanese, saying:

Source 4

Eisenhower recalled this in a magazine interview in 1963.

. . . it wasn't necessary to hit them with that awful thing . . . I hated to see our country be the first to use such a weapon.

Khrushchev said:

Source 5

From a speech in February 1959.

There are only two ways: either peaceful coexistence or the most destructive war in history.

So why didn't they stop the development of these awful weapons? One reason was money. Eisenhower was a Republican whose supporters expected him to cut spending. One way of doing that was to reduce defence expenditure. In the 1950s a ton of high explosive TNT cost $1,700. The amount of nuclear explosives needed to make an explosion of the same force cost only $23. So Eisenhower produced a policy called the 'New Look'. This policy was based on the fact that the United States could use its nuclear superiority to destroy the Soviet Union. It did not need a large and expensive army. This policy enabled Eisenhower to keep the defence budget down to about $40 billion a year.

Khrushchev, meanwhile, was attempting to modernise the Soviet economy. That meant more investment in Soviet factories and less spending on defence. For Khrushchev, too, nuclear weapons offered a cheap alternative to a large and costly army.

Both leaders realised that a nuclear war was unwinnable. The 'policy of deterrence' was based on the idea that if either superpower attacked, the other would retaliate. Hiroshima had shown the horrible effects of a nuclear attack. Both sides were deterred from attacking by the certainty of 'Mutually Assured Destruction', or MAD.

Source 6

The theory of MAD. One side launches a 'first strike' from ground bases/submarines. The other side's radar detects the attack and launches missiles and bombers to retaliate. Both sides are devastated. Both sides also adopted a policy of 'overkill'. That meant stockpiling far more weapons than they needed, so that if some were destroyed in an attack there would still be enough left to retaliate.

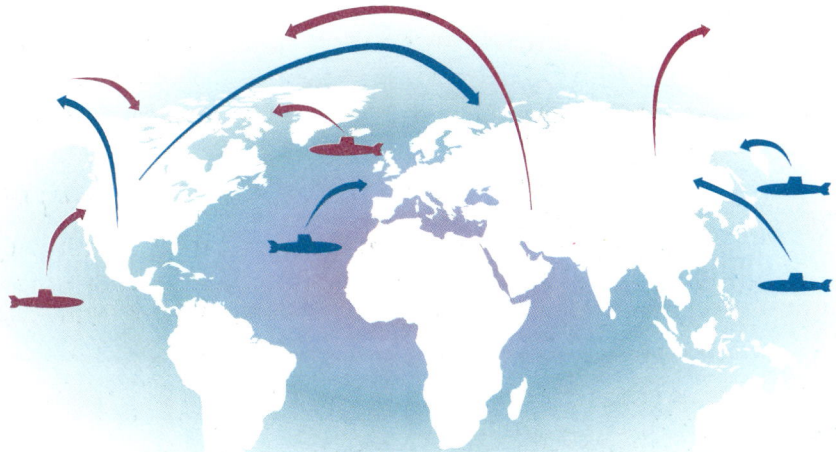

1   What do Sources 4 and 5 show about Eisenhower's and Khrushchev's feelings about using nuclear weapons?

2   Both leaders understood the theory of MAD. Why did they each develop nuclear weapons and threaten to use them?

Even so, both leaders used the threat of the bomb: Eisenhower, to end the Korean War and later to intimidate communist China. Khrushchev talked about using it to drive the Western powers out of Berlin.

The space race

The Hiroshima bomb was delivered to its target by a bomber aeroplane. But heavy bombers were slow and their range was limited. The superpowers wanted more effective delivery systems for their weapons.

The people of Chiswick had found out about a new way of delivering weapons in 1944. The first German V-2 rocket landed on their part of London when it hit the ground causing thirteen casualties. In the six-minute journey from its launch pad the rocket travelled at 3,200 kph and reached a height of 36 km. After the war both the USA and USSR tried to capture scientists and acquire information so that they could take advantage of German rocket technology. This was the start of the space race. By the late 1950s both superpowers were developing missiles capable of carrying nuclear warheads over very long distances. In 1957 the USSR took the lead by firing the world's first Intercontinental Ballistic Missile, or ICBM.

The Soviets achieved another first in 1957 when they fired a satellite, Sputnik, into orbit round the earth. Sputnik itself had no military importance. But it was a turning point in terms of superpower rivalry. The world greeted it as a Soviet triumph. Yet another Soviet success came in

1961 with the first person in space. Yuri Gagarin orbited the earth for 90 minutes. A Russian, Tatyana Iyoderova, said later:

From a British Television documentary on Soviet history shown in 1990.

I can't explain how we felt. There were crowds all over Red Square. Everybody was shouting – Our Yuri in space . . .. It was such a triumph, we were so incredibly happy.

Khrushchev and Nixon discussing the merits of communism and capitalism in 1959.

More important than Sputnik was the huge rocket which boosted it into orbit. The term 'ballistic' implies that a missile is thrown at its target. If the Soviets could throw Sputnik high enough to put it into orbit, they could throw missiles at the United States. Americans suddenly felt very vulnerable. Khrushchev's boasts made the crisis of confidence worse. He was bluffing, but the Americans thought the USSR had achieved strategic superiority. In 1957 American intelligence estimated that the Soviet Union would have 1,000 ICBMs in 1961, to the USA's 70. The figures were wildly exaggerated. But people thought there was a 'missile gap'.

A conflict of ideas

One of the main reasons for the arms race was that the Americans and Soviets had such different ideas about how a country should be run. The Americans believed in 'capitalism'. In a capitalist system people are free to run businesses for profit; they can employ workers and pay them wages. The Soviets were 'Communists'. They thought profits were the result of paying people less than the real value of their work. To avoid that the state should own businesses on behalf of everyone.

An example of this disagreement came into the open in 1959. Khrushchev and Vice-President Nixon were visiting a trade fair. At the American stand – a model kitchen – the two got into a heated discussion (Source 8). They spent an hour arguing over the capitalist and communist systems. This incident became known as the 'kitchen debate'. Many American and Soviet people agreed with their leaders and saw the other side as their enemy.

The conflict of capitalist and communist ideas was an important reason for the superpowers' distrust and fear of one another.

How did ordinary people react to the arms race?

In 1940 Churchill criticised the Germans for bombing civilians. By the end of the Second World War military and political leaders accepted such attacks, as Hiroshima showed. But many ordinary people were appalled – both by the attacks on civilians and the effects of nuclear weapons. In Britain the Campaign for Nuclear Disarmament (CND) was set up to campaign against nuclear weapons. It was more difficult to protest in the United States: during the McCarthy era in the 1950s, 'pacifists' were assumed to be Communists and risked losing their jobs. No protests were allowed in the Soviet Union.

Many people were frightened about what would happen to them if there was a nuclear strike. Carefully selected officials and politicians had places in shelters equipped with all they needed to survive an attack. There were no official shelters for ordinary people. Instead, American TV showed a cartoon featuring a duck and a tortoise with a song telling them to 'Duck and Cover'. So some people had their own shelters installed in their gardens.

■ Do you think you would have wanted a shelter like the one in Source 9? Explain your answer.

Source 9

Inside a fall-out shelter.

earth covering for extra protection against nuclear fall-out

air filter system worked by occupants

access – would have to be well-sealed to stop fall-out penetrating

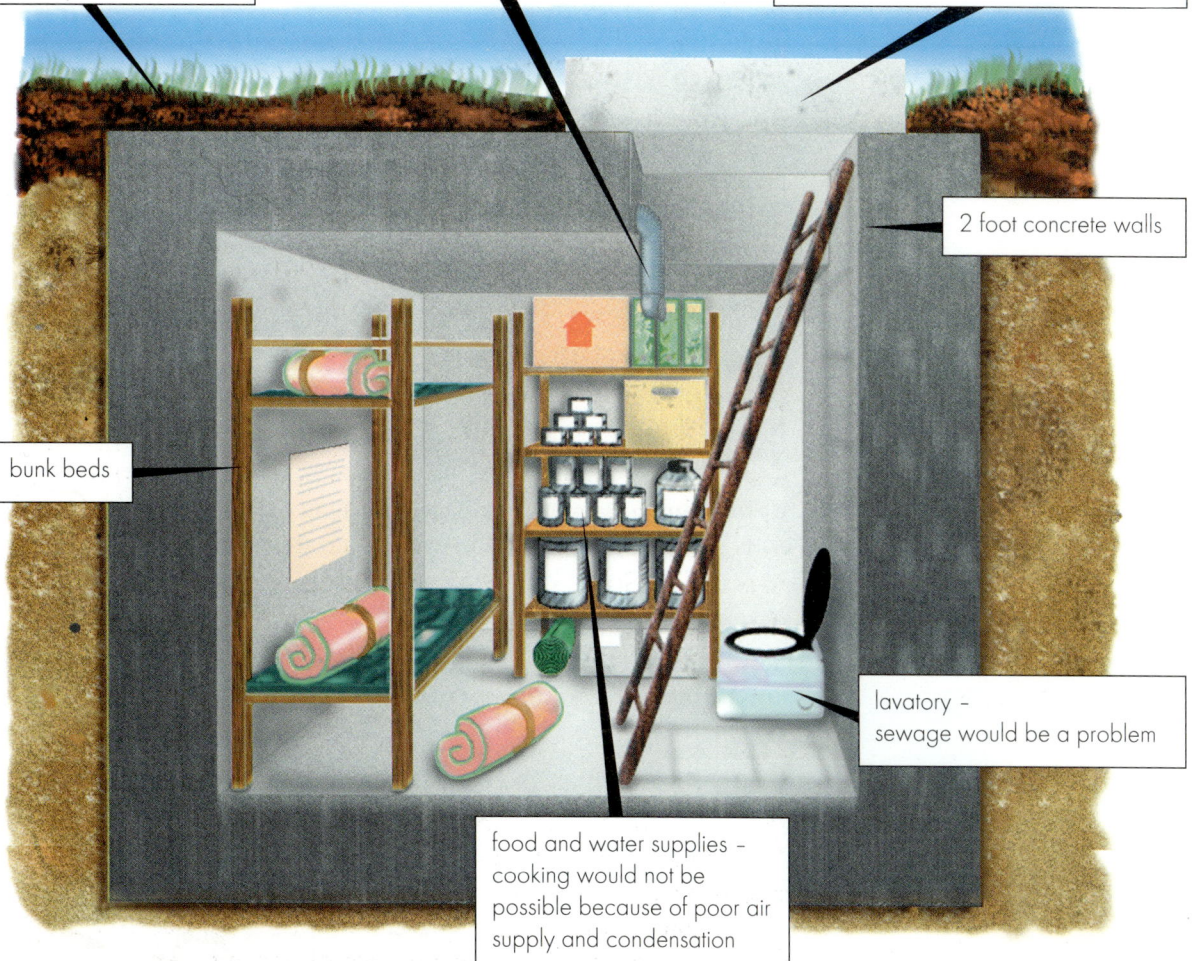

2 foot concrete walls

bunk beds

lavatory – sewage would be a problem

food and water supplies – cooking would not be possible because of poor air supply and condensation

The failure of arms control

Fears about the threat of war led Eisenhower and Khrushchev to begin talks on arms reduction. In 1959 Khrushchev became the first Soviet leader to visit America. The two leaders arranged to meet for a Summit in Paris in May 1960.

Summit   A meeting of world leaders.

On 1 May an American U-2 plane was brought down over the Soviet Union. The United States claimed it was studying the weather but the Russians had captured the sophisticated reconnaissance gear. The pilot, Gary Powers, was imprisoned for spying. A Soviet official remembers what happened in Paris on 16 May:

Source 10

Andrei Gromyko, *Memories*, published in 1989. Gromyko was a former Soviet Foreign Minister.

Khrushchev took the floor: 'This meeting can begin its work if President Eisenhower will apologise . . . for Gary Powers' provocation.'

In a barely audible voice, Eisenhower replied, 'I have no intention of making any such apology, as I have nothing to apologise for,' . . . without uttering a word, everyone got up and left the hall.

It was the end of the Paris Summit. Relations were so bad that American forces were put on world-wide alert.

As a result of this tension there were calls for more arms spending. Soviet academics claimed this was deliberate:

Source 11

From an American study of Soviet views published in the 1970s.

. . . in order to protect its enormous arms appropriations [spending], the Pentagon strives to maintain constant nervous tension in the highest government circles . . . [and arms manufacturers] seek to prevent improved relations with the Soviet Union.

Eisenhower gave this view some support. He warned the United States to guard against letting the defence industry gain too much influence. But during the 1960 election campaign, John Kennedy claimed the USA was not doing well enough in the Cold War. Fears about the missile gap helped take him to the White House.

Questions

1 Look at Sources 10 and 11.
a) Explain the reasons for these disagreements.
b) Use these Sources and any other information you have to explain why the Paris Summit collapsed.

2 **a)** In Source 11, what are the Soviets accusing the Americans of doing?
b) Is there any evidence to suggest that the Soviets were right?

Task

'In my opinion, the Cold War was simply the unrestricted arms race between the superpowers and the state of hostility between them that continually threatened to erupt into a worldwide holocaust.' A comment by Alexei Filitov, a lecturer at Moscow University, in 1992.

Filitov suggests that the Cold War was just about the arms race and the constant threat of war. Use the information in this Unit to explain whether you agree or whether there are other aspects beside the arms race. Write at least a paragraph.

Unit 4 · Kennedy, Khrushchev and Cuba

4.1 Background to the Cuban Missiles Crisis

When President Kennedy took office in 1961, superpower relations were very bad. Eisenhower's and Khrushchev's attempts to control the arms race had failed. But they had resulted in Khrushchev being accused of failing to protect the Soviet Union. He needed a victory to prove that he was an effective leader. In 1961 Khrushchev hoped that the arrival of the young and inexperienced Kennedy as US President would give him the chance to achieve a victory: in Berlin.

Berlin

Source 1

A German family trying to see over the Wall to relatives in the East.

■ Describe the effect of the situation in Berlin in the early Sixties on superpower relations.

Berlin was a problem to the Soviets. The affluent Western sector reminded people how much freer and more prosperous Western Europe was. Between 1949 and 1958 over 2 million East Germans escaped to the West. Gradually the East German government installed barbed-wire fencing, mine-fields and machine-gun posts along the border to stop people leaving. But they could still get out through Berlin.

Khrushchev had been putting pressure on the Western Allies to leave Berlin since 1958. He accused the West of using Berlin as a base for spies and acts of sabotage against the East. He claimed that Berlin was like a powder keg at the end of lighted fuse. An incident there could explode into war. Khrushchev had hoped to reach an agreement with the West over Berlin at the Paris Summit in 1960. But the shooting down of the American U-2 resulted in the collapse of the Summit and a worsening of East–West relations. As tension grew during the first half of 1961, over 100,000 people fled to the West through Berlin. This created serious labour shortages in East Germany. Matters came to a head in an unexpected way. On Sunday 13 August Berliners woke up to find that the city had been cut in two by a barbed-wire fence. A few days later communist troops started building a wall across the city. It divided not just East and West Berlin but also families and friends. People were not allowed to visit the other side of the city. East Berliners with jobs in West Berlin could not go to work. Anyone who tried to get over the Wall risked being shot.

The Americans protested but could do nothing. Kennedy remarked that a wall is better than a war. But he knew the failure to tear down the Wall and stop the USSR imprisoning East German citizens had made him look weak.

Khrushchev, too, appeared weak. His attempts to push the Western Allies out and take control of the whole of Berlin had failed. What could he do now?

Source 2

A West German cartoon about superpower relations which appeared in *The Times* on 1 May, 1962.

THE SUMMIT GETS HIGHER AND HIGHER

Bigger, better bombs: the new arms race

Kennedy came to power wanting to appear strong. He began a huge build up of American weapons, nuclear and conventional. This sparked off a new stage in the arms race because the Soviets responded by increasing their own forces.

After the Berlin crisis Khrushchev took the arms race a stage further. He announced the test explosion of the 'big bomb', 3,000 times more powerful than the one dropped on Hiroshima and larger than anything the US had. Kennedy knew that despite this America was stronger. Even so, critics at home forced him into agreeing to atmospheric tests in April 1962.

So, by early 1962, both leaders were testing nuclear weapons to prove their strength. They had managed to avoid going to war over Berlin. But the Wall which split the city for nearly 30 years left both of them facing accusations of weakness. A showdown was inevitable. It came in an unexpected place: Cuba.

Why was the USA concerned about Cuba?

In 1959 Fidel Castro took power in Cuba. The United States had troops based on the island, and owned most of its wealth. Despite Castro's links with the Communists, the US government decided not to act. The American public welcomed him as a romantic hero.

Castro introduced a land reform programme and nationalised American-owned mines. He asked the Americans for loans to help build up the Cuban economy but they refused. In 1960, the USSR signed an agreement with Cuba to trade sugar for oil and machinery.

By the time President Kennedy took office the United States had broken off relations with Cuba. The CIA was training anti-Castro exiles as part of a plan to invade. One of Kennedy's first decisions was whether or not to approve the invasion of Cuba. He let it go ahead. The exiles landed at the Bay of Pigs and were quickly defeated by Cuban forces.

President Kennedy was so furious at the failure of the Bay of Pigs invasion that he ordered the CIA to find a way to kill Castro. Their efforts included a plan to poison him using capsules smuggled into Cuba in a jar of face-cream. The cream dissolved the capsules! These attempts helped make Castro fearful of the United States. He asked the USSR for military support. In August 1962 the Soviets began secretly shipping equipment and technicians to Cuba. They started building nuclear missile bases there.

Questions

1 Look at Source 2. What does it show about the increasing tension in 1961–1962?

2 Explain why the United States, the world's greatest power, was concerned about what happened in Cuba.

3 Why did Castro turn to the Soviet Union for economic and military support?

4.2 'Gazing down the nuclear gun-barrel'

This section consists of a range of sources from the time of the Cuban Missiles Crisis.   You can use them to carry out research into the crisis, working in a similar way to a historian. It is not quite the same. You do not have to go out and find the Sources and then read all the way through them to find the information you need. But you will have to read between the lines to work out what was happening.

You can use the Sources to try to identify the most dangerous points and the reasons why, despite the danger, the crisis did not end in nuclear war. You can also study people's feelings (those of ordinary people as well as the leaders) as the crisis unfolded. And you can study the roles of the two leaders themselves.

All historians have to select the material that is useful to them for a particular study. You will have to choose what to include – and what to leave out.

Source 3

One of a series of photos taken by United States' U-2 reconnaissance planes from 14 October onwards. They showed short- and long-range missile sites being built in Cuba.

To help him decide what to do about the missile sites, President Kennedy set up a special committee of twelve advisers. It called itself the Executive Committee, or ExComm. Kennedy secretly tape-recorded its discussions.

Source 4

An extract from an ExComm discussion, taken from the TV documentary *The Nuclear Age*, made in 1989. McBundy and McNamara were two of Kennedy's advisers.

McBundy: What is the impact on the United States of MRBMs in Cuba? How greatly does this change the strategic balance?

Kennedy: You may say that it doesn't matter if you get blown up by an ICBM flying in from the Soviet Union or one from ninety miles away . . . What difference does it make? They've got enough to blow us up anyway.

McNamara: I don't believe it is primarily a military problem. It's primarily a domestic political problem.

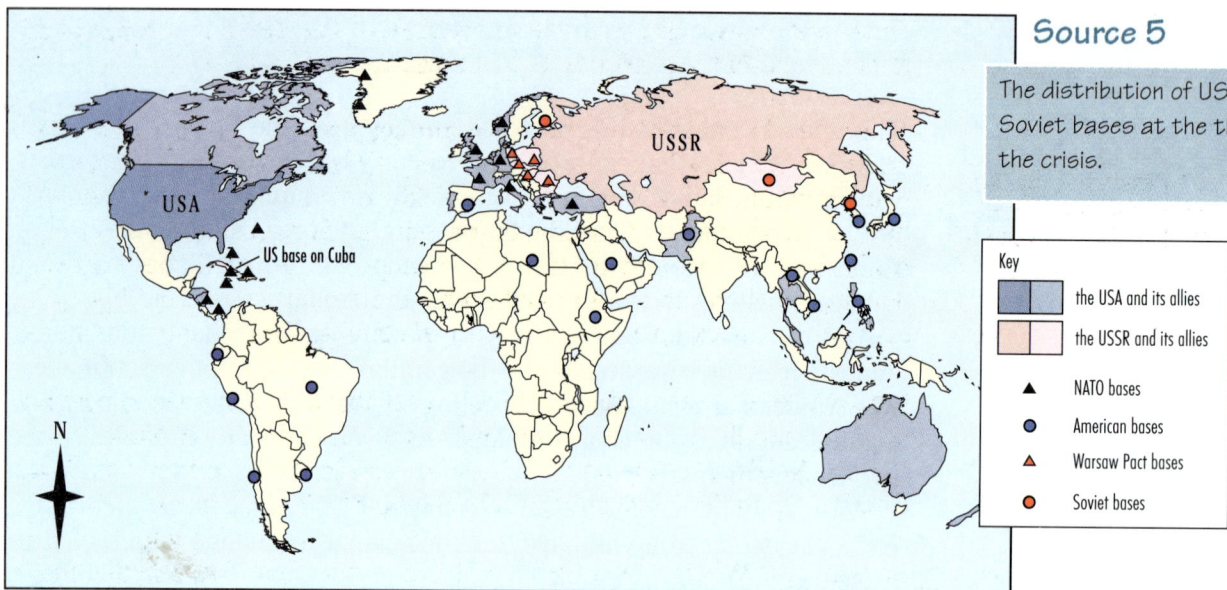

Source 5

The distribution of US and Soviet bases at the time of the crisis.

Andrei Gromyko, Soviet Foreign Minister during the crisis, described a meeting with Kennedy at the White House on 18 October:

Source 6

Andrei Gromyko, *Memories*, published in 1989.

I put the Soviet position to the President. '. . . The American side has conducted an unrestrained anti-Cuban campaign . . .. This course can lead to serious consequences for the whole of mankind.'

Kennedy replied, 'The point is, the present regime in Cuba does not suit the USA.'

I asked him: 'But what basis does the American leadership have for supposing that the Cubans ought to decide their domestic affairs according to Washington's judgement . . . ?'

On 22 October President Kennedy made a televised broadcast to the nation. In it he spoke of:

Source 7

From a broadcast on all three American television networks, 22 October 1962.

. . . this secret, swift and extraordinary build-up of Communist missiles – in an area well-known to have a special relationship to the United States . . . this sudden, clandestine decision to station strategic weapons for the first time outside of Soviet soil – is a deliberately provocative and unjustified change in the status quo which cannot be accepted.

The Soviet government responded in a statement presented to the UN on 23 October:

Source 8

From *Documents on International Affairs*, The Royal Institute of International Affairs, 1962.

Last night Mr Kennedy announced that he had given orders to the US Navy to intercept all ships bound for Cuba . . . in other words, to engage in piracy.

. . . the President's statement shows that the United States imperialist circles will stop at nothing in their attempts to stifle a Sovereign State

. . . to do this they are prepared to push the world towards the abyss of nuclear catastrophe.

. . . the Soviet Union's assistance is exclusively designed to improve Cuba's defensive capability.

Deedra Adams, who was a schoolgirl in 1962, described what she remembered of the crisis in a TV documentary shown in 1992:

Source 9

From the *Timewatch* television documentary on the Cuban Missiles Crisis, shown in 1992.

The schools decided that they would set up air raid drills for the children. So they had a siren and every time the siren went off the teacher would say, 'Okay children, quickly, quickly!' And we would all have to jump under the desk and put our hands over our heads and I really don't know what good that was supposed to have done. But we would stay there, scared to death, until the second siren would go off and we'd get back up and resume normal activities.

Meanwhile, ExComm was discussing what to do if Soviet ships heading for Cuba should fail to stop when ordered to do so by the US Navy.

Both Robert McNamara and Admiral George Waldo Anderson, Naval Chief of Operations remember a conversation on 24 October:

Source 10

From the television documentary *The Nuclear Age*, made in 1989.

McNamara: What do you propose to do when that ship reaches the quarantine line?
Anderson: We propose to stop it!
McN: That's clear, George, but how?
GWA: We'll use our customary methods.
McN: What are those?
GWA: We'll hail it.
McN: What language will you hail it in?
GWA: How the hell do I know? I guess we'll hail it in English.
McN: Suppose you hail in English and they don't speak English. What are you going to do?
GWA: We'll fire a warning shot across their bows!
McN: What if they don't stop then?
GWA: We'll fire a shot through their rudder!
McN: What will happen to that ship if you fire a shot through its rudder?
GWA: Well, it might miss a little bit, it might catch fire . . .
McN: Well, let me tell you something, we are not trying to start a war. There will be NO shot fired by ANYBODY!

Source 11

A US naval vessel (bottom) alongside a Soviet ship with missiles on board as it approaches the quarantine line.

Source 12

An account by one of Kennedy's staff of how he told them what was happening on the quarantine line in the television documentary *The Nuclear Age*.

Source 13

From *Documents on International Affairs*, The Royal Institute of International Affairs, 1962.

Source 14

The Times, 28 October 1992.

Source 15

From the *Timewatch* television documentary on the Cuban Missiles Crisis shown in 1992.

'They've stopped! The ships have stopped! The captain reports they're dead in the water!'

As the crisis deepened, Kennedy and Khrushchev exchanged messages by telegram. Here are extracts from Khrushchev's messages on 26 and 27 October:

. . . we understand that if we attack you, you will respond in the same way . . . and then reciprocal extermination will begin.
   You want to rid your country of danger . . . . But Cuba also wants the same thing . . . you have surrounded the Soviet Union with military bases . . . your rockets are aimed against us . . .. You are worried about Cuba because she lies 90 miles across the sea . . . . But Turkey lies next to us; our sentries pace up and down and watch each other. Do you believe you have the right to demand security for your own country while not recognising it for us?

27 October was 'Black Saturday'. An American U-2 plane was shot down over Cuba by a Soviet SAM missile. Then another U-2 strayed into Soviet airspace. When he heard about that incident McNamara turned white and exclaimed that it would mean war with the Soviet Union. Source 14 gives some indication of how Kennedy responded to this new crisis:

EXPLANATION ON U-2

Mr Kennedy admitted that a U-2 aircraft had violated Soviet airspace
   . . . "I regret this incident," said Mr Kennedy, "and will see to it that every precaution is taken to prevent recurrence."

Source 15 shows how three of those people involved in the crisis later remembered their feelings on 27 October:

15 A An American Naval officer:
We were prepared to immediately start landing troops. We felt it was the real thing and we were scared to death.

15 B A Soviet officer:
I don't know what would have happened to the US invasion forces if the tactical [nuclear] weapons had scored a direct hit. We'd probably have had nothing left to do.

15 C Fidel Castro:
We believed it would turn into nuclear war and our island would disappear.

President Kennedy's brother Robert, the US Attorney General, was the leading member of ExComm. He persuaded his brother to make one last attempt to settle the crisis peacefully.
   In Source 16 Robert Kennedy describes a meeting he had with the Soviet Ambassador on the evening of 27 October:

Source 16

Robert Kennedy, *Thirteen Days: the Cuban Missile Crisis,* published in 1969.

I told him that we knew work was continuing on the missile bases and that one of our U-2s had been shot down and the pilot killed. That was a most serious turn of events . . .

I said that the Soviet Union had secretly established missile bases on Cuba . . . .. We had to have a commitment by tomorrow that those bases would be removed.

He raised the issue of Turkey . . . I said there could be no arrangement under this kind of threat. However, President Kennedy had been anxious to remove those missiles for some time . . ..

On 28 October there was an announcement on Radio Moscow.

Source 17

From *Documents on International Affairs*, The Royal Institute of International Affairs, 1962.

Attention! Moscow calling

The Soviet Government has issued a new order, for the weapons which you describe as offensive to be dismantled and returned to the Soviet Union.

Tasks

You can use these sources in a number of ways. (But remember they won't all be useful for everything.)

1 Use the Sources to make a day-by-day list of events during the crisis. Indicate the most dangerous points in the crisis.

2 Use the Sources to pick out the role of one or both of the leaders. You could put them under headings:

Activities of

Kennedy   Khrushchev

3 Find as much evidence as you can in the Sources about how people felt during the crisis. How much did their feelings vary? Did some people's positions or roles mean they felt differently from others?

4 Study the statement made by the two superpowers and their ministers carefully. In columns, note:

Date: Person speaking: Point made about Cuba:

What do they suggest the crisis was really about?

5 Choose two Sources which are clearly written from opposite points of view. Explain how the fact that they reflect a particular view is useful.

4.3   Aftermath of the Cuban Missiles Crisis

The Cuban Missiles Crisis ended with the Soviets withdrawing their missiles from Cuba. In return the United States promised not to invade the island and gave a secret understanding to pull their missiles out of Turkey. One of Kennedy's advisors later said it had been like gazing down the nuclear gun-barrel and realising that everything you stood for and dreamed of could be blown up. Neither side wanted to come that close to war again.

A major problem during those dangerous days in October was that Kennedy and Khrushchev had to communicate by messages telegraphed between the embassies. It took hours for these messages to travel between Washington and Moscow. (The Soviet Embassy had to give its encoded messages to a bicycle courier who pedalled them down to the Western Union Telegraph Office!) So a 'hot-line' telephone link was installed between the White House and the Kremlin. This meant if there were another crisis, the American and Soviet leaders could speak to each other directly. They began negotiations which led to a partial Nuclear Test Ban Treaty, which was signed in July 1963.

But by the end of 1964 Krushchev had been thrown out of power, Kennedy was dead, and the Cold War was building up again in Vietnam.

Source 18

From the report of a conference in Moscow in the *Guardian,* 30 January 1989. Americans, Soviets and Cubans who were involved in the Cuban Missiles Crisis met to discuss their different views of what happened.

Looking back: an exercise in interpretation

The conference appears to have convinced the American participants that Soviet determination to defend Cuba against American assault played a much larger role in Khrushchev's thinking than has previously been acknowledged. Although Khrushchev cited the defence of Cuba as his primary motive for installing missiles there, US officials and academics have tended . . . to see the crisis strictly as a Soviet–American showdown over an issue of strategic advantage.

Source 19

Stephen Ambrose, *Rise to Globalism* (4th edition), 1985.

The issue in Cuba was prestige . . .. As Theodore Sorensen later put it, 'To be sure, these Cuban missiles alone . . . did not substantially alter the strategic balance in fact . . . but that balance would have been substantially altered in appearance.' The most serious crisis in the history of mankind, in short, turned on a question of appearances. The world came close to total destruction over a matter of prestige.

Questions

1   Read Source 18 carefully. According to the Source, how did the Americans originally see the crisis? How has the American view of the reasons for the crisis changed during the Moscow conference?

2   Source 19 suggests that there was an entirely different reason for the crisis. What was it?

3   Look again at Sources 18 and 19. In your view, which of these sources is the more accurate explanation of what the crisis was about? Support your answer with whatever evidence you can find in this Unit.

Unit 5 · Containment in Vietnam

In 1954 an American flying ace nicknamed 'Earthquake McGoon' was killed in Vietnam. He crashed while flying supplies into the town of Dien Bien Phu. Vietnam has been called 'the war that nobody won'. Why did it happen? And why was the United States involved?

5.1 The early stages, 1954-1965

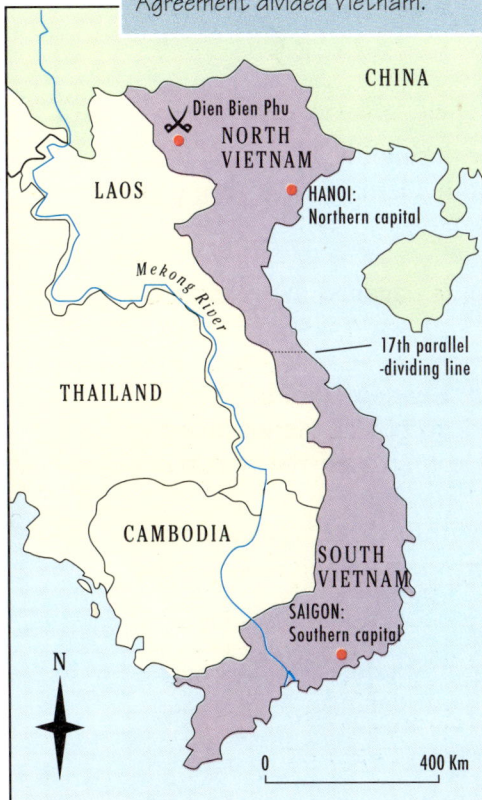

How the 1954 Geneva Agreement divided Vietnam.

Until the Second World War, Vietnam was a French colony. In 1946 Ho Chi Minh, the leader of the Vietnamese Communists, called Vietminh, declared independence. But the French tried to reimpose their authority by force. At first the Americans welcomed 'decolonisation': the break up of the European empires. But when the Communists seized power in China in 1949 they changed their minds. The United States government believed that if Vietnam fell to the Communists other countries would follow.

The US sent 'advisors', such as Earthquake McGoon to help the French. In May 1954, the Vietminh overran Dien Bien Phu, killing or capturing all but 73 of the 12,000 French troops there. This resulted in a cease-fire agreement which divided Vietnam in two – North and South. Neither Ho Chi Minh nor Diem, the Southern leader, accepted this settlement.

The National Liberation Front

In 1960 the Vietminh set up the National Liberation Front, or NLF. It was supposed to be South Vietnamese but was in fact run from Hanoi. Its supporters became known as the Vietcong. The NLF set out to achieve a 'social revolution' in the countryside. They gave the land to the peasants and involved them in the running of their villages. Women in particular benefited from the new system. They had been considered inferior. Now the Vietcong set up Women's Associations to tackle the inequalities. It actively recruited women fighters and had women officers and even generals. Many women supported the Vietcong, acting as soldiers, spies and porters. One of these women, Hoang Thi Me was involved in fighting both the French and Americans. She remembered:

Source 2

Arlen Eisen, *Women and Revolution in Viet Nam*, 1984.

We worked with women in the fields. As we planted we talked about the issues. The women wanted to be active and were very militant because we were struggling for women's rights.

Source 3

General Nguyen Thi Dinh. By 1975 she was Deputy Commander in Chief of the NLF and a third of Vietcong fighters were women.

The Vietcong's work among the peasants contrasted sharply with the behaviour of the South Vietnamese Army (ARVN). It was supposed to protect the peasants from the NLF. But it acted like an occupying force and treated them badly. In 1962 an American report showed that the peasants tended to support the Vietcong.

Kennedy and Vietnam

President Kennedy was an American senator during the 1950s. He made speeches in favour of US support for the South Vietnamese government. He called Vietnam:

Source 4

Extract from comments Kennedy made while he was a senator, from Stanley Karnov, *Vietnam: A History,* 1983.

. . . a proving ground for democracy in Asia . . . against the relentless pressure of the Chinese Communists.

After his embarrassment over the Berlin Wall, Kennedy decided Vietnam would be a good place to demonstrate American power. He promised to help Diem, the South Vietnamese leader. He increased the number of 'advisors' in Vietnam from 700 to 15,000.

In 1963 Diem and Kennedy were shot within three weeks of each other. The new President, Johnson, had visited Vietnam and reported that it was:

Source 5

The Report by Vice President Johnson on his visit to Asian Countries given to President Kennedy in May 1961.

. . . critical to the US . . .. The basic decision in Southeast Asia is here. We must decide whether to help . . . or to pull our defences back to San Francisco and a 'fortress America' concept . . ..

American 'advisors' continued to help the ARVN, for example by using helicopters to fly them into battle. But by 1964 soldiers from the North were filtering through to the NLF. The US decided that the only way to beat them was to send in American troops.

Questions

1 Look at Sources 2 and 3. Can you suggest why the Vietcong should have made a point of working with women?

2 Why should most peasants have preferred the Vietcong to their own government?

5.2 The USA at war, 1965–1973

The CIA set up an incident to make it look as though the North Vietnamese were planning to invade the South. This 'attempted landing' was reported in the newspapers (Source 6). It gave Johnson the excuse to launch 'Operation Rolling Thunder', the first air attack against the North. Then, in March 1965, 3,500 combat troops landed openly at Da Nang to join the 23,000 Americans already in Vietnam. Finally, in May, Johnson declared all Vietnam a combat zone.

Source 6

From *The Times'* report of the incident the CIA set up, 1 February 1965.

■ The newspaper report, Source 6, is based on 'misinformation' provided to the newspapers by the CIA. How does that affect its value as a source?

ATTEMPTED LANDING

Saigon Jan. 31. – South Vietnam has informed the International Control Commission of an attempted landing of North Vietnamese troops . . . police fired on the Communists and captured one soldier, a boat and also arms and ammunition.

Kosygin, the new Soviet Prime Minister, was trying to persuade Ho Chi Minh to consider negotiations when the US troops arrived. Neither the Russians nor the Chinese were keen to support him in a war against the United States, but neither wanted the other to accuse them of being 'soft on capitalism'. So Kosygin promised Ho military aid. Although the Soviets and Chinese gave the North far less support than America gave the South, they competed with each other to send weapons and equipment.

The number of US troops in Vietnam increased rapidly. But there were never enough to fight the NLF effectively. The Americans' first problem was to find the enemy. The Vietcong were spread out through the countryside. They came together for surprise attacks, then scattered. American units went out on 'search and destroy' missions to try to locate them, but very few resulted in a proper fight with the enemy.

This was intensely frustrating for the soldiers. Most of them were conscripts, with an average age of only nineteen. Even worse was not being able to tell who was the enemy. A Marine commander remembers two men being killed by a youngster they were teaching to play volleyball. Another Marine remembered:

Source 7

William Ehrhart, quoted in Stanley Karnow, *Vietnam: A History*, 1983.

. . . the enemy would disappear and you'd end up taking out your frustrations on the civilians . . . Any Vietnamese seen running away was a Vietcong suspect. One day I shot a woman in a rice field because she was running . . . sixty years old, unarmed . . . I didn't think twice about it.

An Army nurse summed up the feelings of despair in a letter home:

Source 8

First Lieutenant Lynda Van Devanter wrote this in 1969. It is quoted in the film *Dear America*, which largely features letters home from Americans serving in Vietnam.

Christmas came and went, marked only by tragedy . . . I'm tired of going to sleep and listening to rockets, mortars, artillery. I'm sick of facing every day a new bunch of children ripped to pieces. They're just kids – 18, 19, their whole lives ahead of them, cut off. I'm sick to death of it.

Peace, Lynda

Public opinion turns against the war

Vietnam was the first war to be fought on television. In August 1965, TV viewers were shocked to see a GI casually setting fire to a peasant hut with his 'Zippo' lighter. In 1968 they were horrified to watch a Vietcong captive being shot dead at point-blank range. Such images helped to turn world opinion against the war. Robert McNamara warned Johnson:

Source 9

From a 1967 memorandum. Johnson sacked McNamara shortly afterwards.

There may be a limit beyond which many Americans and much of the world will not allow the United States to go. The picture of the world's greatest superpower killing or seriously injuring 1,000 non-combatants a week, while trying to pound a tiny, backward nation into submission . . . is not a pretty one.

Source 10

A man holding a napalmed child.

Many Americans did not understand what the Vietnam War was about. They were appalled by the losses. In 1967, 160 men a week were killed, returning to the USA in 'body bags'. People were also concerned about the costs. Johnson had promised that he would build the 'Great Society' and put an end to inequality and deprivation. As the war sucked money away from domestic programmes, black Americans were among those who turned against it. Only twelve per cent of the US population was black. But as one Civil Rights group said in a statement:

Source 11

The Civil Rights Movement and War in Vietnam, published in 1966.

We maintain that our country's cry of 'preserve freedom in the world' is a hypocritical mask . . . 16 per cent of the draftees from this country are negro, called on to preserve a 'democracy' which does not exist for them at home.

By 1968 thousands of men and women, young and old, were taking part in anti-war demonstrations. The 'protest movement' was underway.

Source 12

Anti-war demonstrators sit down at Berkeley, one of America's smartest colleges.

The Tet Offensive attacks.

Key
→ The Ho Chi Minh trail, the NLF supply line to the South
★ major battles
▨ prolonged confrontation

CHINA
Dien Bien Phu
LAOS
HANOI
NORTH VIETNAM
Khesanh
17th parallel -dividing line
Da Nang
Mekong River
THAILAND
CAMBODIA
N
SAIGON SOUTH VIETNAM
0   400 Km

The Americans lose heart

Early in 1968 a major NLF build-up near an American base at Khesanh led to 5,600 Marines becoming surrounded. President Johnson declared that Khesanh would not be given up. He had a model of the area built in the White House basement and went down at night to prowl round it in his bathrobe. There were rumours that nuclear weapons would be used. US planes dropped 5,000 bombs in the area every day: the equivalent of five Hiroshima bombs. The Marines spent 76 days under siege and 500 men were killed. At last, in April, American troops broke through to the base and lifted the siege. In June the US abandoned Khesanh – secretly, so that the American people should not know that the lives lost there had been for nothing.

Meanwhile, on 30 January Vietcong forces launched the 'Tet Offensive'. They simultaneously attacked the South's major cities and towns. In Saigon a suicide squad seized the US Embassy and had to be driven out by paratroopers landing on the roof. It took 11,000 troops a whole week to force the Vietcong out of Saigon. One soldier, interviewed for TV as he reloaded his rifle during the fighting, said:

From an American television news report in 1968.

Just hope you can stay alive from day to day. I just want to go back home . . . the whole thing stinks really.

The Americans defeated the Vietcong at Khesanh and in the Tet Offensive. But they suffered an even bigger defeat themselves. The Vietcong lost 80,000 fighters but the US Army lost its credibility. They had won these battles but they could not win the war.

Johnson had to pull out of the 1968 Presidential race because the war was so unpopular. His successor, Richard Nixon, promised to bring the troops home.

The United States pulls out

Nixon kept his promise and started pulling out US troops in 1969. The ARVN had to take over. To help them Nixon increased the air raids. During one eleven-day bombardment of Hanoi 2,000 people were killed. US planes sprayed defoliants, including 'Agent Orange', over huge areas of forest to uncover NLF supply lines. They doused villages with napalm to 'flush out' the Vietcong. Nixon secretly ordered the bombing and invasion of neutral Cambodia to stop supplies coming down the Ho Chi Minh Trail (see Source 15).

During this process of 'Vietnamisation', survival became the name of the game among US troops. No one wanted to be the last person to die in a pointless war. By 1970, soldiers were wearing peace symbols and refusing to go into battle. In 1970 alone 207 officers were killed by 'fragging': their men rolled fragmentation grenades into their tents, blowing them to pieces. At last, in 1973, the negotiations which had been dragging on for five years resulted in agreement. The Americans pulled out, leaving the South Vietnamese to fight on alone. The ARVN could not hold out for long. On May Day 1975 the Vietcong captured Saigon and the war was over.

But at a terrible cost.

Questions

1 Look at Source 10. How does the photograph explain what McNamara is saying in Source 9?

2 Using Source 11 explain why many black Americans objected to the war.

3 Look at Source 12. Why should women have objected to the war?

5.3   Consequences of the Vietnam War

The 'Cold War' was given that name because of the idea that there was no actual fighting between the superpowers. But the Americans became involved in Vietnam because of their determination to stop the spread of communism. The Soviet Union and the Chinese supported the Vietcong in their fight against the US forces. The following Sources and information show some of the consequences of the war for both the American and Vietnamese people who were caught up in it. Study them and then tackle the Tasks.

Source 15

Veterans at the memorial to the American war dead in Washington.

Source 16

The aftermath of a 'search and destroy' mission.

Dr Nguyen Thi Phuong, an obstetrician, commented after the war on birth defects at her hospital:

Source 17

Imagine how we feel. Couples who have been separated by many years of war finally reunite. Some of the women get pregnant. Then the new born child dies because of severe genetic malformations resulting from the parents' exposure to defoliants. We have many, many such cases.

Source 18

Military waste still littering Khesanh in 1993. This area used to be tropical rainforest: it was reduced to scrub by the bombardment.

Both sides paid a heavy price for the Vietnam war. It cost the US $120 billion. Of the 3 million men and women who served there, 58,000 were killed and many more injured. Some 700,000 veterans, women as well as men, have suffered psychological effects: it has been shown that they are far more likely than the rest of the population to experience panic attacks, depression, drug addiction and to be divorced or unemployed. More veterans have committed suicide since coming back than were killed in Vietnam. The Americans lost faith in their ability to 'contain' communism.

For the Vietnamese people the impact of the war was far worse. Two million men, women and children were killed and many more injured. Millions were driven from their villages, their homes, crops and livestock destroyed. Over seven million tons of bombs were dropped on Vietnam, more than three times the total dropped in the Second World War. They reduced vast areas to moonscapes of burnt trees and craters. Millions of gallons of defoliants laid waste yet more of the country, causing irreversible damage to the tropical rainforest. Vietnam was reduced from a major exporter of rice to a country which could not even feed itself. An American trade embargo has made it very difficult for Vietnam to rebuild its economy. The suffering of its people were largely ignored during the war and are mostly forgotten today.

Tasks

1 Look back through this Unit on the Vietnam War and make a list of the advantages and disadvantages the Vietcong had over the Americans (e.g., fighting in their own country but less well-equipped). Do the same for the Americans.

Then consider Stephen Ambrose's view that the Americans were: '. . . cocky, overconfident . . . certain they could win at bearable cost, and that . . . they would turn back the Communist tide in Asia.' (From his book, *Rise to Globalism*.) Use your list to decide how accurate an explanation this is of why the Americans failed in Vietnam.

2 Choose a range of headings for the different types of consequences of the war, e.g. environmental effects, effects on the South Vietnamese people. Use the information and Sources to make list of consequences under these headings. Then write a report of the war, divided into sections under the headings you have chosen. Sum up your report by saying what you think of the war and why.

Unit 6 · Defusing the tensions, 1968–1979

By the late 1960s relations between the superpowers were very bad. Americans were fighting in Vietnam against troops who were using Soviet supplies. And there were new developments in the arms race.

6.1   The arms race, 1968–1972

There were two major advances in nuclear weapons technology by this time: ABMs and MIRV. In 1966 the Russians started to build an anti-ballistic missile (ABM) system, code-named Galosh. It was supposed to protect Moscow from attack by missiles. It could never have worked but it set some Americans thinking. Why not build systems to protect American cities? Other thinkers said ABMs would not work and would be very expensive. They also argued that if the superpowers had ABMs to defend themselves, it might make them less frightened of launching a nuclear attack. They would not need to fear MAD if they could destroy missiles fired in retaliation.

Source 1

The ABM theory.

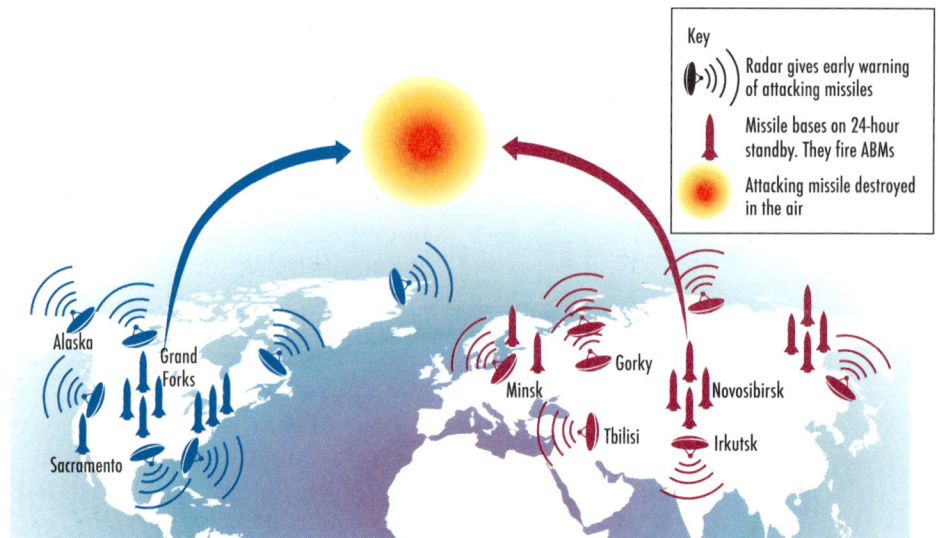

Key

Radar gives early warning of attacking missiles

Missile bases on 24-hour standby. They fire ABMs

Attacking missile destroyed in the air

Alaska   Grand Forks   Sacramento   Minsk   Gorky   Novosibirsk   Tbilisi   Irkutsk

■ The Soviets developed an ABM system first. Why should they have been alarmed that the Americans decided to develop one as well?

MIRV stood for 'multiple independently targeted re-entry vehicle'. These missiles could carry up to ten warheads, each aimed at a different target. This development greatly increased the fire power the American weapons could aim at the USSR. In 1968 the USA decided to go ahead and develop both ABMs and MIRV.

Why did the superpowers want detente?

The Soviet Union was thoroughly alarmed by the American decision to develop ABMs. They had other worries too. Soviet industry could send people into orbit and land vehicles on the moon. But it was otherwise very inefficient. In the late 1960s a leading scientist wrote:

Source 2

Andrei Sakharov, *Progress, Co-existence and Intellectual Freedom.* Sakharov was the 'father' of the Soviet H bomb.

We are now catching up with the United States only in some of the old, traditional industries which are no longer as important as they used to be . . . .. In some newer fields, for example, automation, computers and especially in industrial research and development, we are not only lagging behind, but are also growing more slowly.

Brezhnev, the Soviet leader, realised that somehow he had to tackle the USSR's economic problems. He decided to do this by co-operating with the West. But that meant trying to reduce tension. So the USSR announced its willingness to discuss arms limitation.

The Americans and Russians agreed to start talks. They prepared a joint announcement to be released on 21 August 1968. On 20 August, Warsaw Pact forces ousted the Czech government which had been trying to introduce democratic reforms. The United States called off the talks and started testing MIRV.

■ Both Nixon and Brezhnev had their own particular reasons for wanting detente. What were they?

Source 3

An American cartoon about the reasons for SALT, published in 1970.

SALT

Richard Nixon became President of the United States in 1969. Nixon's main concern was to get the United States out of the Vietnam War. He hoped to do this by persuading the Russians and Chinese to stop supporting North Vietnam. He saw arms control as a bargaining chip to get the Soviets out of Vietnam. So Strategic Arms Limitation Talks began in November. During the three years of negotiations Nixon refused to allow discussion of MIRV. He was determined that the US should stay ahead in the arms race. Meanwhile, in 1971 Brezhnev announced a 'Programme for Peace'. He said it was intended to put into practice the ideas of peaceful coexistence.

Nixon also tried to improve relations with China. At last, in 1972, the United States officially recognised the Chinese government and agreed to let them join the UN. The Soviets were alarmed at the possibility of China and America ganging up on them. Brezhnev invited Nixon to Moscow and in 1972 they signed the SALT I Interim Agreement and an ABM Treaty. An American expert wrote:

Source 4

Stephen Ambrose, *Rise to Globalism* (4th edition), 1985. This study of US foreign policy was first published in 1971.

The SALT I agreement froze ICBM deployment but not MIRV, which was about as meaningful as freezing the cavalry of European nations in 1938 but not the tanks.

Throughout the Nixon administration the Pentagon added three new warheads a day to the MIRV arsenal. It was a strange way to control the arms race.

As well as SALT, the two sides signed a trade agreement allowing America to export grain to Russia. They encouraged artistic and sporting links, hoping that this would lead to greater understanding. In 1975 Soviet and American astronauts linked up in space.

Source 5

Weapons increases after SALT I.

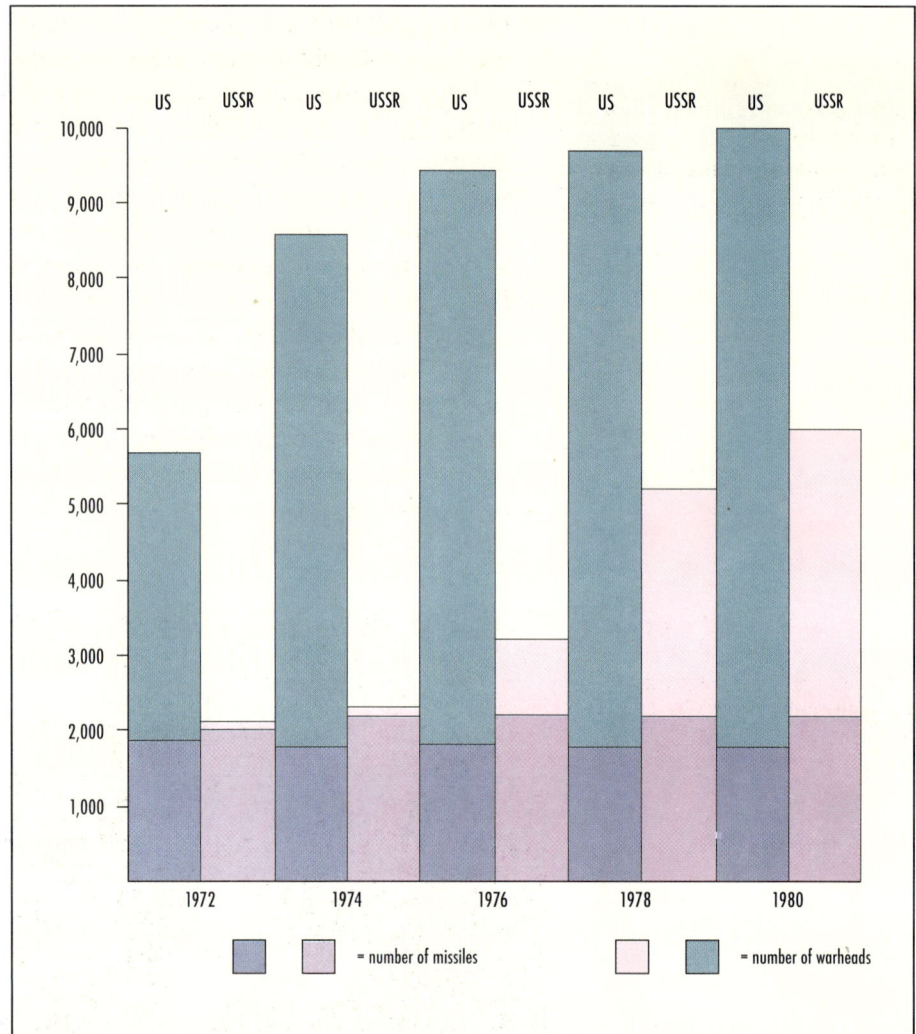

	US	USSR	US	USSR	US	USSR	US	USSR	US	USSR
10,000										
9,000										
8,000										
7,000										
6,000										
5,000										
4,000										
3,000										
2,000										
1,000										
	1972		1974		1976		1978		1980	

= number of missiles   = number of warheads

Questions

1 What does the cartoon Source 3 suggest were the reasons for SALT?

2 Study Sources 4 and 5. How far does Source 5 support Professor Ambrose's comment in Source 4?

6.2   Detente, 1972–1979

Brezhnev's 'Programme for Peace' included detente in Europe. The Soviets signed treaties recognising West Germany as a country. They allowed West Berliners to visit relatives in East Berlin. In 1975 35 countries, including the United States and the USSR, signed the Helsinki Agreement. In it the West recognised Soviet dominance of Eastern Europe. Each side agreed to notify the other of military exercises and allow them to send observers. All 35 countries agreed to:

Source 6

The Helsinki Accords, 1975.

. . . respect human rights and fundamental freedoms, including the freedom of thought, conscience, religion or belief for all without distinction as to race, sex, language or religion.

Dissident The term used for Soviet people who criticised their government in the 1970s and 1980s.

In 1975 Jimmy Carter became President of the USA. He was an idealist. He wanted to eliminate nuclear weapons from the Earth and said human rights were the soul of his foreign policy. The Soviet government was clamping down on 'dissidents' such as Sakharov. Carter criticised them for doing this. The Soviets replied that the unemployment and poverty some Americans suffered was also a denial of human rights. SALT talks continued, but Carter tried to force the Soviets to improve by linking agreements on arms control to human rights. This delayed the signing of SALT II.

In December 1979, before SALT II was ratified in the United States, Soviet troops swept into Afghanistan. Moscow claimed they were invited in by the government there, but the United States denounced this 'invasion' of an independent country. As the USSR started a ten-year war which became known as the Soviet Vietnam, President Carter called on the world's athletes to boycott the Olympic Games which were held in Moscow in 1980. Detente was dead.

Source 7

Carter and Brezhnev exchange signed copies of SALT II in June 1979.

Explain how a) the Americans and b) the Soviets could be accused of breaking the Helsinki Accords.

Task

Make a list of the successes and failures of detente. Then draw a graph of the period from 1968–1979. Mark on it the successes and failures from your list. Times when there are successes are the high points; times when the superpowers disagree are low. Then join up the points with a line: it will end at the bottom of the graph!

Unit 7 · How did superpower rivalry end?

7.1 The Cold War, 1979–1987

Ronald Reagan became US president in 1980, promising to make America strong again. He did not disguise his hatred of communism, calling the Soviet Union 'the Empire of Evil'. The possibility of nuclear war between the superpowers seemed greater than ever. The early Eighties became known as the 'new Cold War'.

Source 1

How Ronald Reagan saw the world, from an American newspaper cartoon published in 1982.

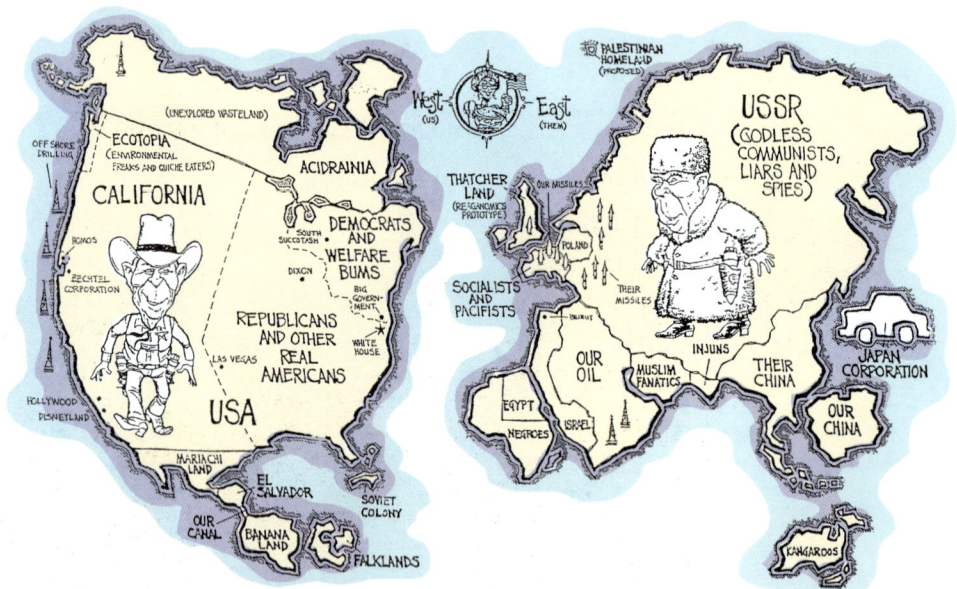

■ Explain what the cartoonist in Source 1 is suggesting about Ronald Reagan's view of the world.

Reagan increased arms spending and pushed the deployment of new intermediate-range missiles. These weapons were very accurate. They were small, so they could be moved around to hide them from the enemy. They were low flying, so they could evade detection by enemy radar. And they were deployed in Europe.

Source 2

How the new missiles were deployed in Europe.

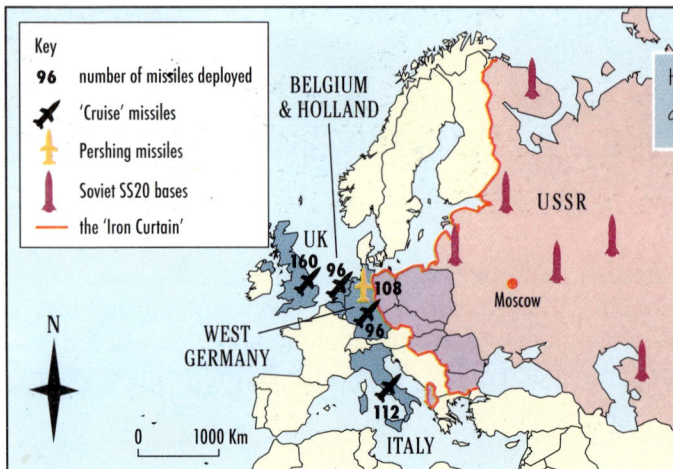

Key
96 number of missiles deployed
✈ 'Cruise' missiles
† Pershing missiles
Soviet SS20 bases
— the 'Iron Curtain'

Throughout the Sixties and Seventies protest had continued against nuclear weapons. But now people became even more alarmed.

Source 3

Stephen Ambrose, *Rise to Globalism* (4th edition), 1985.

To many Europeans . . . it appeared that the United States and the Soviet Union had agreed that if war ever came between them, Europe was to be the battleground . . .. If that happened, then there surely would be no more Europe . . . There was wide-spread alarm and good cause for it.

There were mass demonstrations across Europe. In Britain CND membership surged and protesters joined hands to link the American and Soviet Embassies in London.

In the United States, too, there were huge demonstrations. People were no longer cowed by McCarthyism. There were even attempted demonstrations against nuclear weapons in Moscow.

By now the superpowers had enough weapons to destroy the world many times over: the equivalent of at least three tons of TNT for every person on earth. The costs of the Cold War were crippling both superpowers. It could not go on.

Source 4

British demonstrators trying to block the way to the Cruise Missile base at Greenham Common in the early 1980s.

Questions

1 Use Source 2 to explain the 'alarm' referred to in Source 3.

2 Look carefully at Source 4. What effect do you think this sort of demonstration might have had on the government?

7.2   The end of the Cold War

In 1985 Mikhail Gorbachev became Soviet leader. He knew the USSR was bankrupt. It simply could not afford the arms race. Reagan too faced a huge debt problem. Both had to reduce costs. The United States spent $300 billion on defence in 1983 alone.

Reagan had always been passionately anti-communist. But now, like Gorbachev, he wanted improved relations. This was partly because of his wife. She spent months persuading him to soften his attitude towards the Soviets. As a result Reagan agreed to meet Gorbachev. They got on well together.

Source 5

The Reagans and Gorbachevs meeting in Geneva in 1985. Nancy Reagan was 'very helpful' in pushing for this summit.

The two leaders had another, very strange meeting in 1986. They almost agreed to eliminate nuclear weapons, but ended up with no agreement at all. Afterwards an advisor warned Reagan that:

Source 6

Quoted in *The Nuclear Age*, a history of the arms race, published in 1989.

"We've got to clear up this business about you agreeing to get rid of all nuclear weapons."
   "But, John," replied Reagan, "I did agree to that."
   "No," persisted Poindexter, "you couldn't have."
   "John," said the President, "I was there, and I did."

These discussions resulted in total confusion. But both sides had offered to cut their nuclear arsenals. At last the INF Treaty was signed. This was a turning point, because for the first time the superpowers agreed to get rid of a range of nuclear weapons. The much-feared Cruise, Pershing and SS-20 missiles were withdrawn.

Source 7

The introduction to the 1987 INF Treaty.

The United States of America and the Union of Soviet Socialist Republics . . .
Conscious that nuclear war would have devastating consequences for all mankind,
Guided by the objective of strengthening strategic stability,
Convinced that the measures set forth in the Treaty will help reduce the risk of the outbreak of war and strengthen international peace and security,
Have agreed . . .

Both sides made further proposals to reduce the level of conventional forces as well as nuclear weapons. But events were running ahead of the leaders. In 1989 a wave of anti-government protest swept across Eastern

Europe. This time Moscow did not send in troops. A Soviet spokesman told television reporters:

Source 8

Gennady Gerasimov, of the Soviet Foreign Ministry, speaking in the autumn of 1989.

The new doctrine is in its place which is Frank Sinatra doctrine. Frank Sinatra doctrine has a very popular song, 'I had it my way'. So Hungary, Poland, any other countries has it its own way. They decide which road to take. It's their business.

This astonishing reversal of Soviet policy led to the collapse of communist control. In November the Berlin Wall, the very symbol of the East–West divide, was opened. After a confused announcement, people gathered at a crossing point chanting 'Take the Wall down! Take the Wall down!' An East German, Erich Knorr, saw the border guards pouring out. He thought there was going to be trouble.

Source 9

From *Despatches from the Barricades,* a book about 1989 by John Simpson, a BBC reporter.

But the guards ignored the crowd. They fanned out in front of the post and started shifting the heavy blocks of concrete that lay across the street to prevent cars from passing through more than one at a time. The gates opened. An officer made a gesture with his hand, like a doorman at a hotel . . . the way to the West lay open. Everyone cheered and shouted and sang, and they surged forward, ten abreast.

Source 10

East and West Berliners meet on the Wall, November 1989.

Gorbachev and George Bush, the new American President, met in Malta in December 1989 and declared that the Cold War was over.

The end of superpower rivalry

Even after 1989 the two sides still distrusted each other. Talks on arms reduction went slowly. But events in Russia were moving fast. There were free elections in 1990 and after an attempt to overthrow him in August 1991, Gorbachev outlawed the Communist Party. That December the flag of the newly established Russian Federation replaced the Red Flag over the Kremlin. The Soviet Union had ceased to exist and superpower rivalry was at an end.

Questions

1   Study Source 7. What does it say were the reasons for the INF Treaty?

2   Why does Gennady Gerasimov's statement in Source 8 mark such an important change in Soviet policy towards the countries of Eastern Europe?

3   How does Source 9 show that Soviet policy really had changed?

Task

Look back through this book and find all the events you can which took place in Berlin or affected the city and its people. Look especially at the 1940s, the early 1960s, the beginnings of detente and 1989. Write a history of Berlin during the Cold War. Show how the events which affected Berlin reflected the changing relationship between the superpowers.

7.3 The Cold War legacy

The Cold War left behind a range of problems. One is the environmental damage. Weapons testing has resulted in widespread radioactive contamination, especially in the Pacific and Kazakhstan. Another is cost. Eisenhower pointed out:

Source 11

From a speech made in 1953, pointing out the costs of modern weapons.

Every gun that is made, every warship launched, every rocket fired signifies . . . a theft from those who hunger and are not fed, those who are cold and not clothed.

The Cold War diverted money away from Johnson's 'Great Society'. It helped destroy the Russian economy. And it had a terrible impact in the developing world.

   The problem of nuclear weapons remains. The Non-proliferation Treaty was supposed to stop the spread of nuclear weapons. But many countries have developed their own bomb. The Cold War is over, but there could still be a nuclear war.

Source 12

A British cartoon published in *Punch*, 1969.

Source 13

Countries known or thought to have the capability to make nuclear weapons up until 1991.

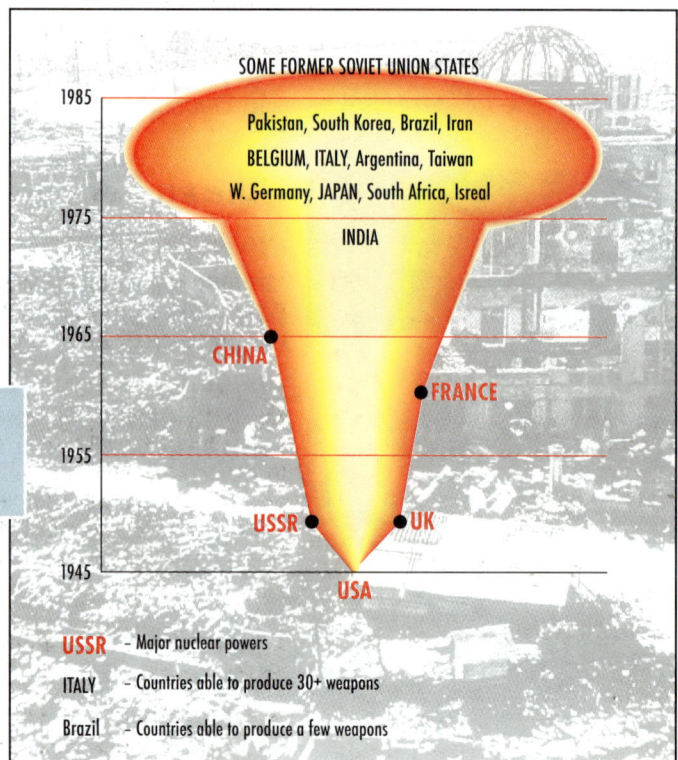

SOME FORMER SOVIET UNION STATES

1985

Pakistan, South Korea, Brazil, Iran
BELGIUM, ITALY, Argentina, Taiwan
W. Germany, JAPAN, South Africa, Isreal

1975

INDIA

1965   CHINA   FRANCE

1955

                         USSR   UK

1945

                         USA

USSR – Major nuclear powers

ITALY – Countries able to produce 30+ weapons

Brazil – Countries able to produce a few weapons

Questions

1 Look at Source 12. What is it saying about the space race? How far does it agree with what Eisenhower's view in Source 11?

2 What other problems have resulted from the Cold War besides the ones referred to in these Sources? Look back through the book if you cannot remember.

3 Now that you have studied the Cold War, do you think the name is right or not? Explain your answer.